The ancient Hawaiian sport of surfing is one of Hawaii's gifts to the world of sports. The original surfboards were made of native Hawaiian wood, carved from a single tree, and could be 18 feet or longer, 5-6 inches thick, 2 feet wide, and weight 150 pounds or more.

Pule Ho'opōmaika'i no Barack Obama, Pelekikena o 'Amelika

E ke Akua mana loa e ho'omaika'i 'oe,
E ho'opiha kou na'au me ke aloha pau'ole,
'O kēia aloha i hō'ike mai ka 'ike loa,
No ka maluhia a me ka lōkahi,
No ka po'e a pau loa ma ka honua.
'Āmama.

by Healani Youn

Healani Youn is a Kumu Hula & Recipient of the
Merrie Monarch's Miss Aloha Hula Title

English Translation:
BLESSING FOR BARACK OBAMA, PRESIDENT OF AMERICA
May the Almighty bless you and fill your heart with deep, endless love,
May this love guide you to the knowledge that brings peace and unity to all people on earth.
The blessing is finished, the words are released.

ISBN 978-0-9800063-0-8

Library of Congress Control Number: 2009902390

Quote on opposite page by Michelle Obama from
Obama: From Promise to Power (HarperCollins Books, 2007)

Banana Patch Press
PO Box 950
Hanapepe, HI 96716
Telephone 1-808-335-5944
Toll-free 1-800-914-5944
www.bananapatchpress.com

Printed in Hong Kong

A President

"You can't really understand Barack until you understand Hawaii."
MICHELLE OBAMA

by Dr. Carolan
& Joanna Carolan

Audio CD:
Amy Hanaialiʻi
with **Keliʻi Kāneali'i**

President Obama
was born in Hawaiʻi,
a first in
America's history.

"...when I look back on my years in Hawaii, I realize how truly lucky I was to have been raised there."
– *Barack Obama, Punahou Bulletin, Fall 1999*

Kama‘āina

He is a **kama‘āina**,*
Hawai‘i-born, or resident.
Will this help him to be
a good President?

*Kama‘āina is the
Hawaiian word for *native-born*;
the literal translation is *land child*;
kama‘āina also means *host* and
is used when referring to
Hawai‘i residents.

"I'm going to go
bodysurfing at an
undisclosed location."
– Barack Obama
Honolulu, HI 8/8/08

Do
you
wonder,
What is it like
to grow up there?
Are there surfers
and hula dancers
everywhere?
GROM

FIRST
DUKE
HAWAII'S ORIGINAL LEI DAY SONG
MAY DAY IS LEI DAY
IN HAWAII
DEDICATED TO THE LEI QUEENS OF HAWAII
PUBLISHED BY
SUMMERS
HAWAII
WHAT THE LEI MEANS
A STORY FROM HAWAII
WORDS AND MUSIC BY ALFRED PEREZ
Composer of "THATS WHAT THE LEI SAID TO ME"

What does it mean to give a flower lei?

A Lei is:
a garland or necklace; it can be made from flowers, shells, leaves or other materials.
A lei is given as a symbol of affection or respect & to acknowledge special occasions.

HAWAII
PREZ 44
ALOHA STATE
HAWAII DRIVER LICENSE USA
H00782801
3.DOB 08/04/1961
4b.Exp 08-04-2016
15.Hgt 6-01
16.Wgt 190
18.Hair BLK
17.Eye BRN
13.Sex M
01/20/2009
3
OBAMA, BARACK HUSSEIN
1600 PENNSYLVANIA AVE
WASHINGTON, DC 20500
ORGAN DONOR
TheBus

Rainbow
DRIVE-IN
Aloha
from Hawaii
Is it true
you can see
a rainbow
every day?

Poi Dog
"We have two criteria that have to be reconciled. One is that Malia is allergic... There are a number of breeds that are hypoallergenic... our preference would be to get a shelter dog....So whether we are going to be able to balance those two things... is a pressing issue in the Obama household."
— Barack Obama 11/7/08

Will he
choose
a
poi dog
as the
white
house
pup
?
In Hawai'i a mutt or mixed-breed dog is called a *poi dog*.

Some
aloha shirts
would sure brighten
things up!
got aloha?
"There will be brighter days ahead."
– Barack Obama, Los Angeles, CA 3/19/09

THE WH USE
PRESIDENT OF THE UNITED
got
aloha?

Let's go to Hawaiʻi
and check it out.
Let's see what it's all about.
A chain of islands makes up our
50th state. Count the main ones –
there are eight. The capital of
Hawaiʻi is **Honolulu.**
It's on the island of
Oʻahu.

UNITED STATES OF AMERICA
MAUI
AWE
HAWAII
(BIG ISLAND)
"Every year,
my family and I
take a Christmas
trip to Hawaii..."
— Barack Obama
PUNAHOU BULLETIN
FALL 1999

President Obama grew up in Makiki, a couple of miles from Waikiki. He lived in these apartments, and scooped ice cream at Baskin-Robbins®; minimum wage was two-dollars and forty-cents.

"There was a court nearby... I'd dribble down there and shoot... I fell in love with the game, played it all through high school... basketball was a refuge, a place where I made a lot of my closest friends, and picked up a lot of my sense of competition and fair play."

– Barack Obama, Sports Illustrated 5/21/08

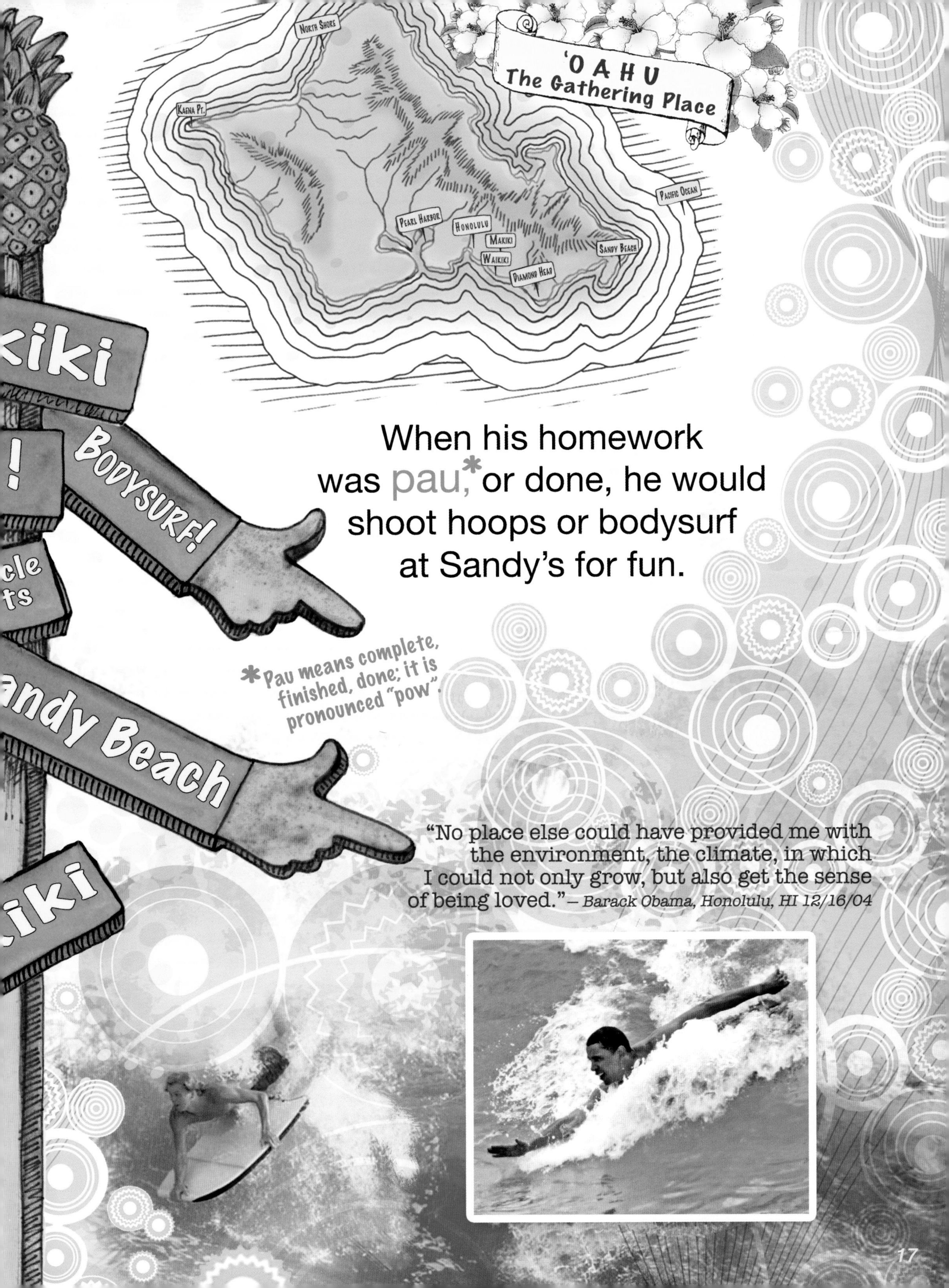

When his homework was pau,* or done, he would shoot hoops or bodysurf at Sandy's for fun.

* Pau means complete, finished, done; it is pronounced "pow".

"No place else could have provided me with the environment, the climate, in which I could not only grow, but also get the sense of being loved." *– Barack Obama, Honolulu, HI 12/16/04*

Here is where our President went to school. Studying hard and getting good grades is very cool.

"There was something about this place and this school that embraced me, gave me support, gave me encouragement and allowed me to grow and to prosper,"
— Barack Obama, Punahou, Honolulu, HI December 17, 2004

kamai
HOW TO BE A GREAT PRESIDENT
"We know that an education is everything to our children's future.
– Barack Obama
Chicago, IL 6/15/08
HISTORY
"Dream big dreams...
- Barack Obama
Punahou, Honolulu, HI
12/17/04
PUNAHOU
...there is so much out there that you can be curious about and learn about."
– Barack Obama
Punahou, Honolulu, HI
12/17/04
HARVARD
ECONOMICS
"...even though my mother didn't have a lot of money, scholarships gave me the chance to go to some of the best schools in the country." – Barack Obama
Manchester, NH 11/20/07
When someone is smart we say they are akamai. President Obama is one akamai guy.
HARVARD
VE RI TAS
"No government program can turn off the TV, or put away the video games, or read to your children." – Barack Obama, Dayton, Ohio 9/09/2008
HARVARD
RVARD
W REVIEW
akamai: smart, clever, skilled, expert

It's important to know some of Hawaii's history
The first Polynesians arrived by sea.
They fished in the ocean, lived
in grass huts and climbed
up the palm trees to
get coconuts.

Sustainable (sə·stā·nə·bəl) *adj* 1 : living in a manner that can be continued without exhausting natural resources or causing ecological damage.

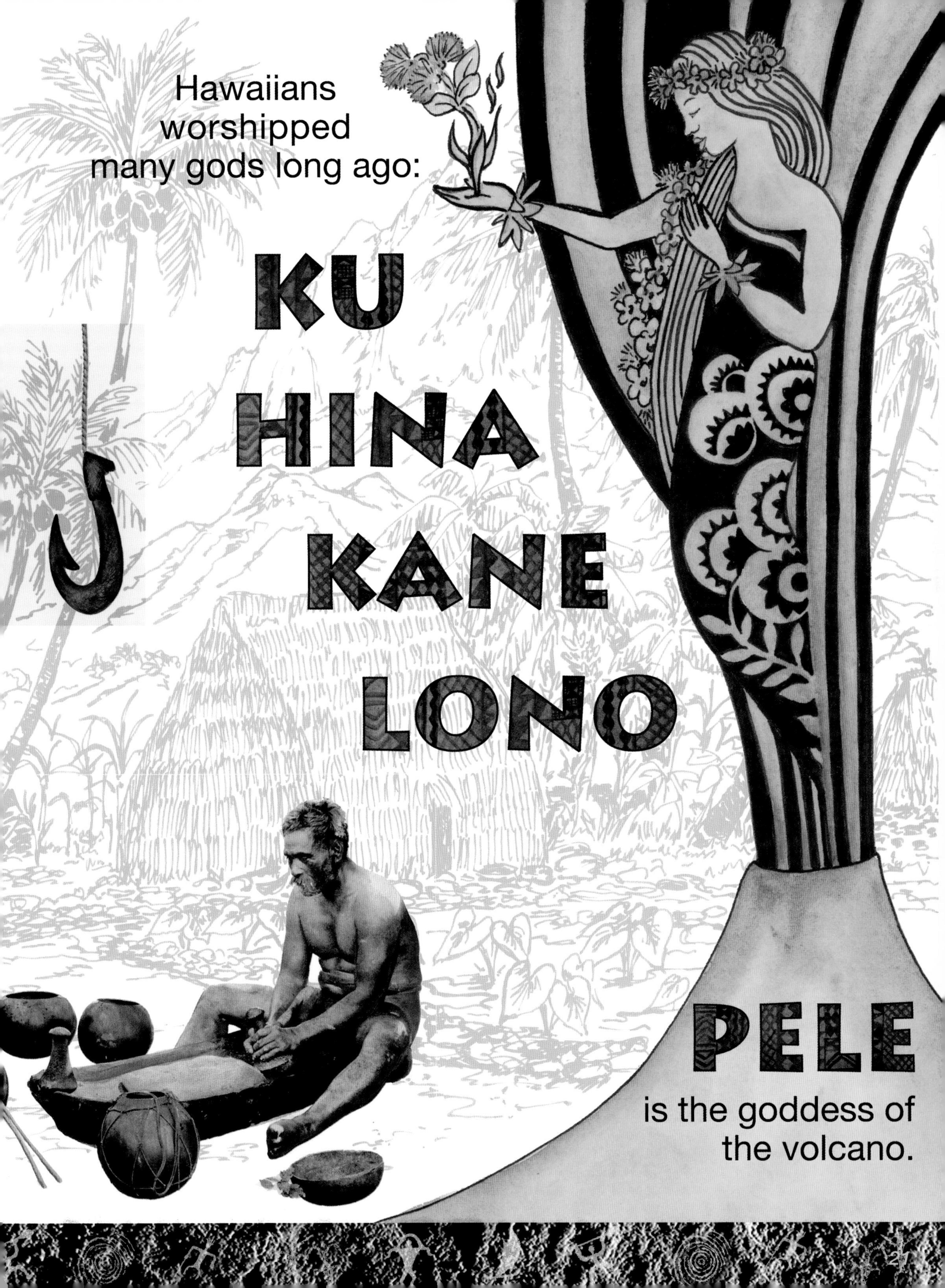

Hawaiians worshipped many gods long ago:

KU

HINA

KANE

LONO

PELE

is the goddess of the volcano.

Some of Hawaii's history is sad.
But good things happened
along with the bad.

Honolulu Star-Bulletin

SMALLPOX!
EPIDEMIC RAVAGES ISLANDS

Commercial Advertiser

QUEEN DEPOSED!

Commercial Advertiser

ANNEXATION!

CERVERA'S FLEET IS ANNIHILATED

"HERE TO STAY!"

And the star-spangled banner
In triumph shall wave
O'er the Isles of Hawaii
And the homes of the brave

The Honolulu Advertiser

GOLD MEDAL FOR HAWAII!
DUKE KAHANAMOKU WINS OLYMPIC GOLD,
SETS NEW SWIMMING WORLD RECORD

Honolulu Star-Bulletin 1st EXTRA

WAR!
OAHU BOMBED BY JAPANESE PLANES

SAN FRANCISCO, Dec. 7.—President Roosevelt announced this morning that Japanese planes had attacked Manila and Pearl Harbor.

STATEHOOD!
House Sends Bill to Ike

Honolulu Star-Bulletin

The Honolulu Advertiser
HAWAI'I'S NEWSPAPER
WEDNESDAY

OBAMA
HAWAI'I'S OWN MAKES HISTORY

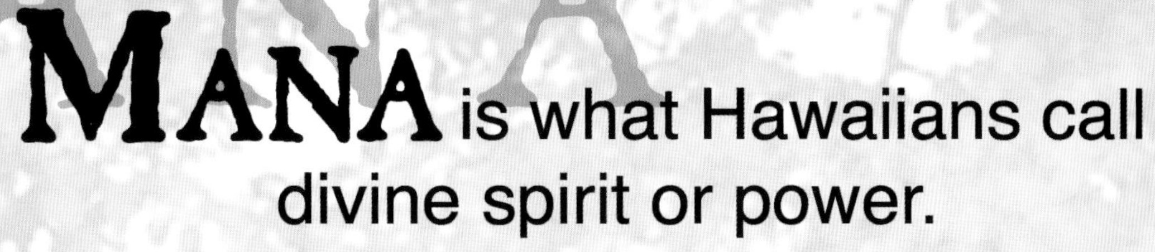

MANA is what Hawaiians call
divine spirit or power.
They believe it is in every person,
rock and flower.

KING KALAKAUA

QUEEN LILIUOKALANI

PRINCESS KAIULANI

Hawai'i had a monarchy;
it was taken away,
but their
mana was strong
and still is today.

Hawai‘i has abundant sunshine and rain, the perfect climate for growing sugarcane.
AVISO
Aos Contribuintes
収税課布告

The sugarcane industry grew at such a fast pace; immigrants came from all over the place:

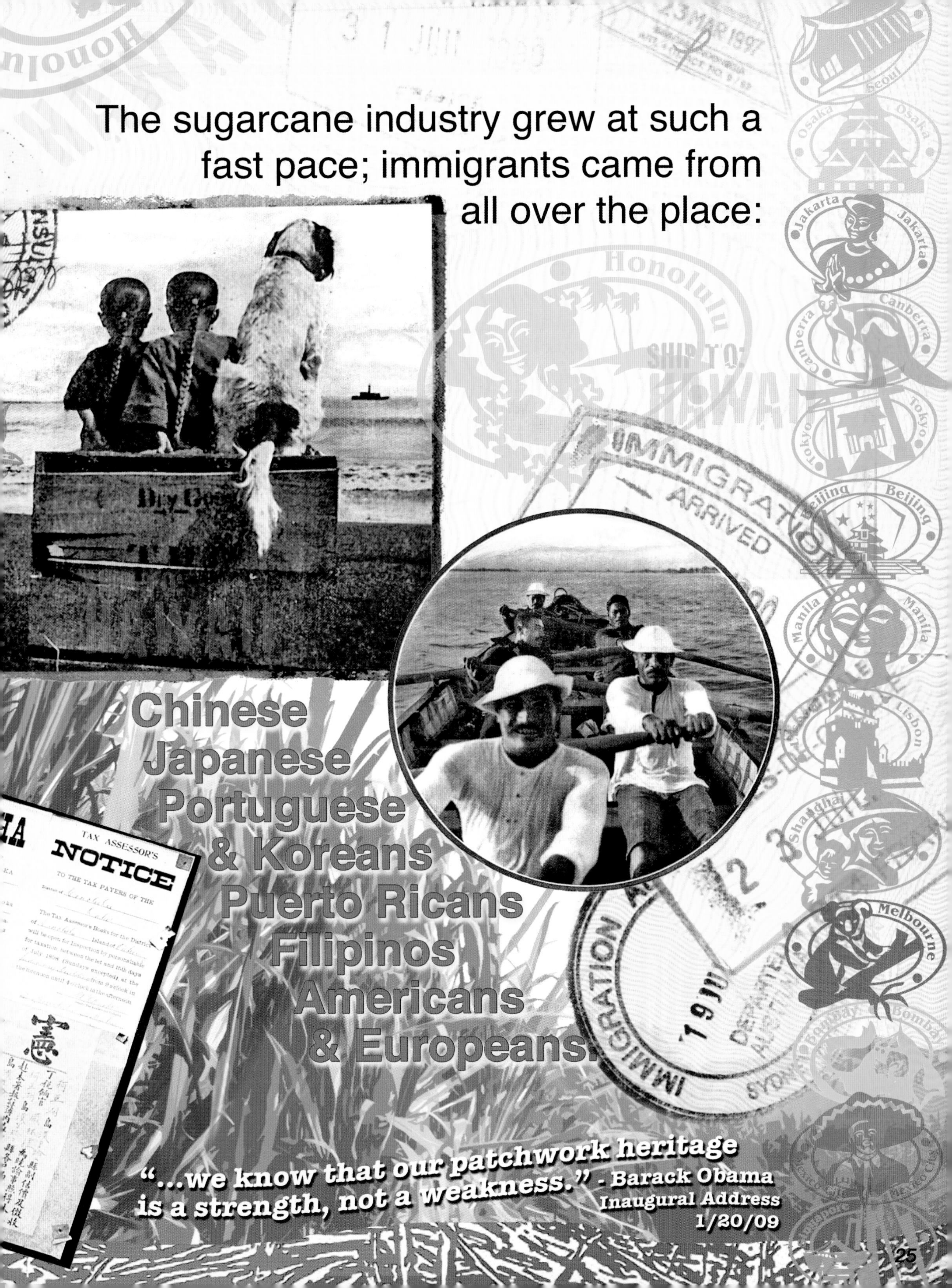

"...we know that our patchwork heritage is a strength, not a weakness." - Barack Obama
Inaugural Address
1/20/09

Each culture added to the melting pot:
Different foods, religions, and ways of thought

"When I was growing up...we would go to a Hawaiian potluck and a Japanese wedding or meet some Portuguese friends...you'd learn to appreciate different cultures and different styles."
– Barack Obama, U.S. News & World Report 5/30/08
POI
Lau Lau
SPAM
Shave ice
"I'm going to get a plate lunch... I'm going to go get some shave ice."
– Barack Obama
Honolulu, HI 8/8/08
COME
OP RICE
AC SALAD
EENS
PLATES
ORK
IMENTO
N MEAT
R CUTLET
PLATES
TI
ER STEAK
CO
W
NG WITH FRIED SAIMIN ADD 1.00

IMAGINE
PEACE

In the middle of the Pacific,
Hawai‘i is just a dot.
And we live close together
in this small spot.
With all our diversity,
how do we live together
peacefully?

"As a child of a black man and a white woman,
someone who was born in the racial melting pot of Hawaii,
with a sister who's half Indonesian...
and a brother-in-law and niece of Chinese descent...
I've never had the option of restricting my loyalties
on the basis of race, or measuring
my worth on the basis of tribe."
— Barack Obama, *The Audacity of Hope*

"...what's
best in me,
and what's best
in my message is
consistent with the
tradition of Hawaii."
– Barack Obama
Honolulu, HI 12/16/04
Aloha

Hawaiian culture & tradition play a big part. Living with **aloha** means giving from the heart. It is a gesture of aloha to give a flower lei. Showing kindness is the aloha way.

"That's why we pass on the values of empathy and kindness to our children by living them."
— *Barack Obama, Chicago IL 6/15/08*

Lōkahi

is another important thing,
like striving for harmony when we sing.
Lōkahi means looking for ways to agree;
it is about creating unity.

"On this day we gather
because we have chosen
hope over fear, unity of purpose
over conflict and discord."
— Barack Obama, Inaugural Address 1/20/09

"...no frontier
is beyond our reach
when we're united,
and not divided."
— Barack Obama, Washington, D.C. 1/28/08

Lōkahi: unity, harmony, agreement, ac

Lōkahi is working together in unison; it takes teamwork and cooperation.

"... it must be about what we can do together..."
— Barack Obama, Springfield IL 2/10/07

Early Hawaiian Temple
circa 1790

Long ago, missionaries came to Hawai'i from far and wide.

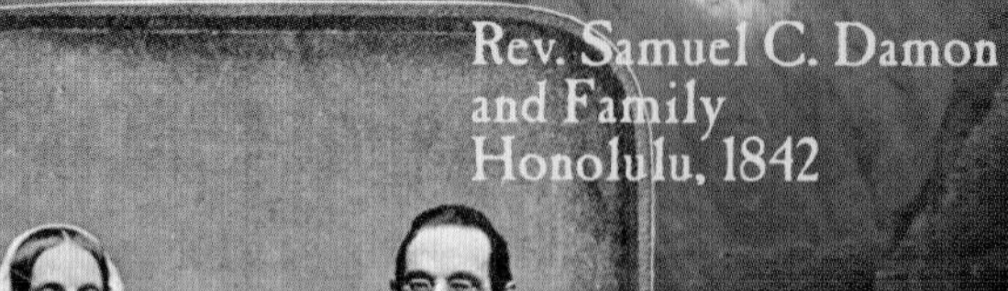

Rev. Samuel C. Damon
and Family
Honolulu, 1842

Byodo-In Temple, Kaneohe

Central Union Church, Makiki

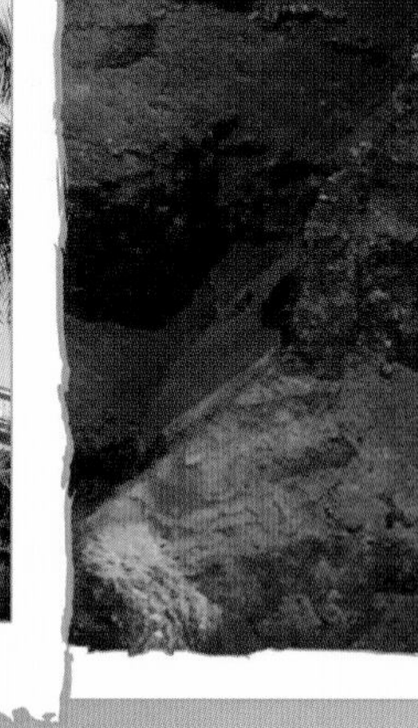

First Chinese Church of Christ, Honolulu

Church of the Crossroads, Honolulu

Today, people of all faiths live here side by side.

Our Lady of Peace
Catholic Church
Honolulu, 1843

Kawaiahaʻo, First Native Church
Honolulu, 1838

On these islands

that are so small, the Hawaiian people made room for them all.

Shinshu Kyokai Buddhist Temple, Makiki

Mormon Church, Makiki

Korean Church, Makiki

Mokuʻaikaua Church, Kailua-Kona

"Faith is not just something you have, it is something that you do."
– Barack Obama 12/1/06

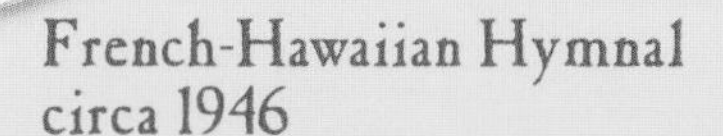

French-Hawaiian Hymnal
circa 1946

*Tūtū

"We call my grandmother Tutu, Toot for short, it means 'grandparent' in Hawaiian..."
— *Barack Obama, Dreams from My Father*

"She's the one who taught me about hard work. She's the one who put off buying a new car or a new dress for herself so that I could have a better life. She poured everything she had into me." — *Barack Obama, DNC Denver, CO 8/28/08*

Kupuna: ancestor, grandparent, repected elder

But whether we are
Christian, Jewish, Muslim,
Hindu, or followers of Buddha,
Hawaiian culture tells us:

Honor our elders, our kūpuna.

Our kūpuna give us guidance
and affection, like his Tūtū *
guided our President in
the right direction.

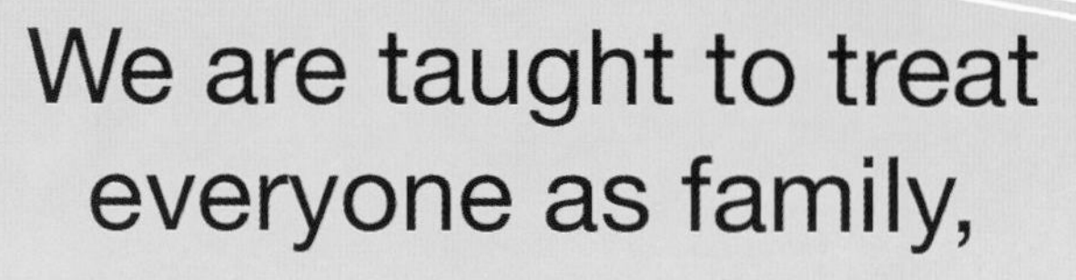

We are taught to treat
everyone as family,
'ohana,
even if they have
a funny name,
like Barack Obama.

"...the hope of a skinny kid with a funny name,
that America has a place for him, too."
– Barack Obama, DNC Boston MA 7/27/04

"The essence of Hawai'i has always been that we come from far and wide,
that we come from different backgrounds and different faiths
and different last names, and yet we come together
as a single 'ohana because we believe in the
fundamental commonality of people."
– Barack Obama, Honolulu, HI 12/16/04

"Of all the rocks upon which we build our lives,
we are reminded today that family is the most important."
— *Barack Obama, Chicago, IL 6/15/08*

"These children are our children.
Their future is our future."
— *Barack Obama, Manchester NH 11/20/07*

Mahalo

is one of the first words we are taught. It means respect and thank you. We say it a lot.

Everyone is called

Auntie or **Uncle**

when you're small.
And each of our **keiki***
is cherished by all.

"...we look out for one another...we deal with each other with courtesy and respect. And most importantly, when you come from Hawai'i, you start understanding that what's on the surface, what people look like, doesn't determine who they are."
— *Barack Obama. Honolulu, HI, 8/8/08*

*Keiki: *child*

SURF

*ʻĀina
Land
Earth
"…I can retrace the first steps I took as a child and be stunned by the beauty of the islands… The moss-covered cliffs and cool rush of Manoa Falls, with its ginger blossoms and high canopies filled with the sound of invisible birds… The shadows off Pali's peaks; the sultry, scented air."
— Barack Obama, Dreams from My Father
*Mālama
Care
Protect

The ʻĀina,

the land, is very important here. On an island, every part is dear.

"...growing up in Hawaii, not only do you appreciate the natural beauty, but there is an ethic of concern for the land that dates back to native Hawaiians."
— Barack Obama, interview U.S. World & News Report 5/30/08

Mālama

means preserving its fragile beauty. Protecting and caring for the ʻāina is our duty.

"We need your service, right now...
I'm going to ask you to play your part..."
- Barack Obama, Colorado Springs, CO 6/2/08

"Individual responsibility and mutual responsibility – that's the essence of America's promise."
— Barack Obama
DNC 8/28/08

"What is required of us now is a new era of responsibility... we have duties to ourselves, our nation, and the world..."
— Barack Obama
Inaugural Address 1/20/09

Duty and responsibility:
Kuleana, is what we say.
It's your **kuleana** to do
your part each day.

Ha'aha'a means being humble.
Don't talk stink; don't grumble.

No Vote No Grumble
www.hawaiianvote.org

No talk stink

Don't be manini; don't be selfish.

REDUCE
REUSE
RECYCLE

"I want us to think about the long term and not just the short term..."
– Barack Obama, ROLLING STONE MAGAZINE 7/10/08

Don't be a litterbug.
Pick up your rubbish.

It only takes a minute to pick up some trash.
And a bottle or can you can recycle for cash.

"My years in Hawaii make me more attuned to certain issues — the environment being a good example."
– Barack Obama, U.S. NEWS & WORLD REPORT 5/30/08

Going for a ride on your bike is good.
Walk around your neighborhood.
Plant a tree. Turn off a light.
Take the bus.
TheBus
BUS INFORMATION
Ph: 848-5555
ALOHA TheBus
Global warming
affects all of us.
"...that means actually starting
to have an energy policy
in this country
that makes sense."
– Barack Obama
Honolulu, HI 8/8/08
Become a community
organizer in your area.
But remember...

"I remembered the stories
that my mother and her parents
had told me as a child...I listened to
my grandmother, sitting under a mango tree
as she braided my sister's hair..."
– *Barack Obama, Dreams from My Father*

...take time to smell the plumeria!
There are a lot of things we have to do,

but it’s important to
hang loose and talk story, too.

When we help
each other, it's a lot more fun.
Kōkua means helping get something done.
Turn off the TV, look around, get involved.
We need to **kōkua** to get
our problems solved.

"That's what this is about...
it's about helping people."
— Barack Obama, Address to Congress
February 24, 2009

KŌKUA: HELP, AID, ASSIST

See how everyone pulls together at a **hukilau?** Our President needs us all to pull together now.

"...all of us can work together, and all of us can join together to create a better country."
– Barack Obama, Honolulu 8/8/08

PPORT

You can help by showing aloha,
rain or shine, with just a
smile or shaka sign.

Aloha may not make all our
problems disappear, but
above the clouds,
the sky is clear.
Here in Hawai‘i,
one thing
we know:
You
must
have
rain
to
get a
rainbow!

"We will come out on the other side
stronger and a more prosperous nation."
— Barack Obama, Los Angeles, CA 3/19/09

"...people ask me, they say, 'What do you still bring from Hawaii?'...
I try to explain to them something about the
aloha spirit... And it's that spirit that I am
absolutely convinced is what America is
looking for right now."
— Barack Obama
Honolulu, HI 8/8/08

"...this country is more than a collection
of Red States and Blue States..."
– Barack Obama, El Dorado, KS 1/29/08
cowboy hula
aloha oe
cowboy hula
aloha oe
"...there is not
a liberal America
and a conservative America -
there is the United States of America.
There's not a Black America and a White America
and Latino America and Asian America -
there's the United States of America."
– Barack Obama, DNC Keynote Address 7/27/04

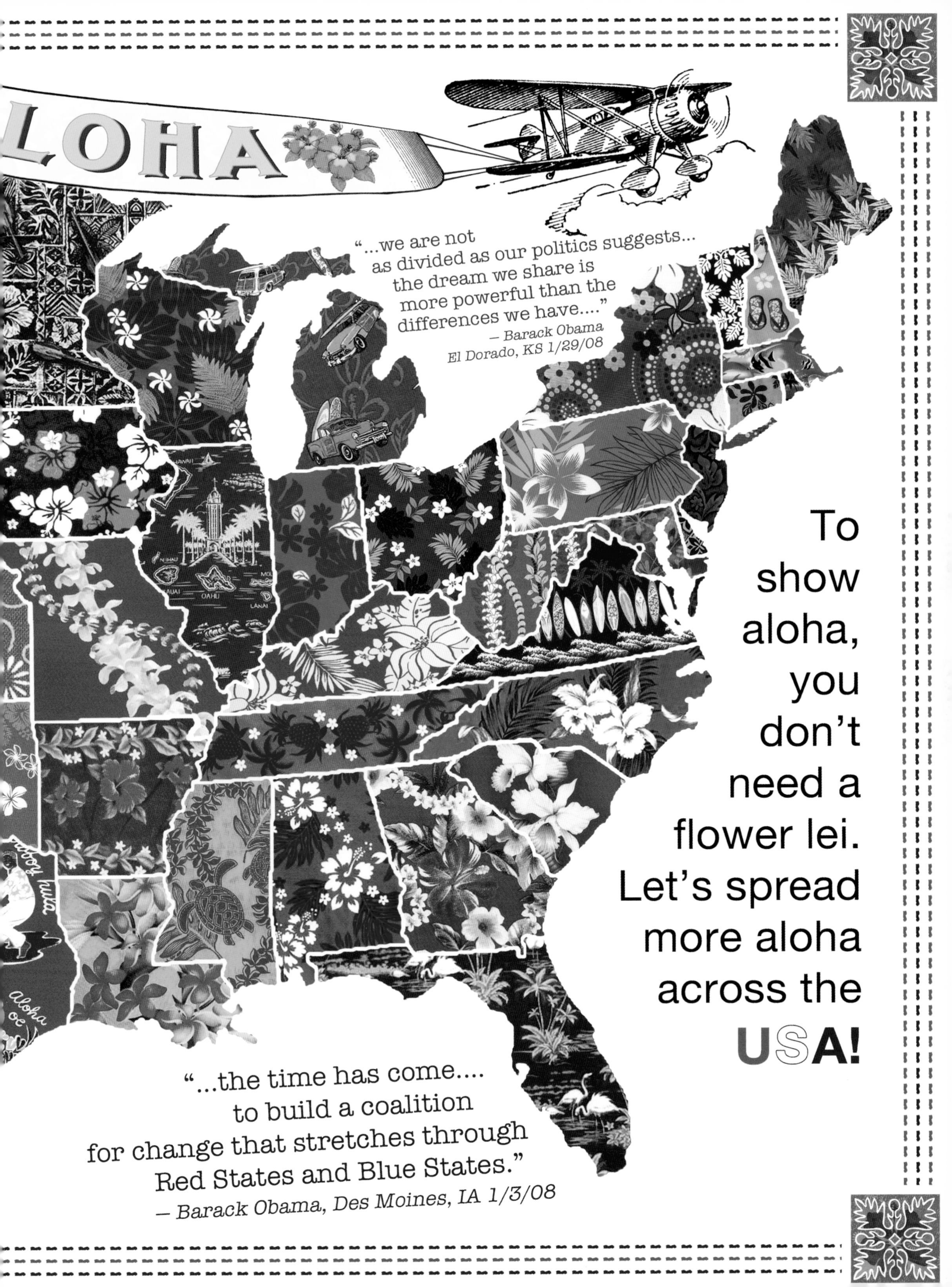

LOHA
"...we are not
as divided as our politics suggests...
the dream we share is
more powerful than the
differences we have...."
– Barack Obama
El Dorado, KS 1/29/08
To
show
aloha,
you
don't
need a
flower lei.
Let's spread
more aloha
across the
USA!
"...the time has come....
to build a coalition
for change that stretches through
Red States and Blue States."
– Barack Obama, Des Moines, IA 1/3/08

PONO means fair, just and good,
with everything going the way it should.

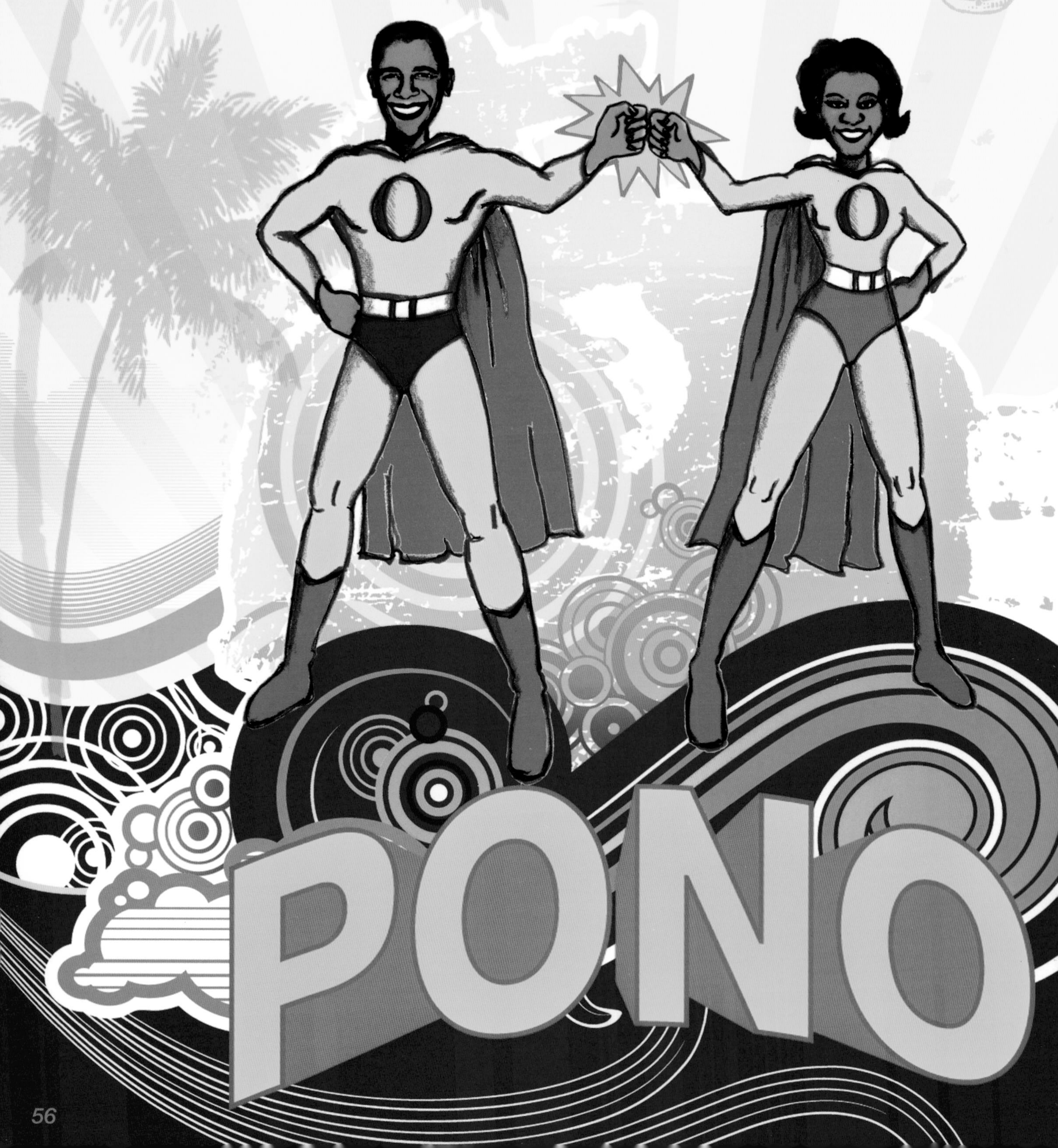

HO'OPONOPONO
is working things out.
Resolving conflict, talking,
listening, forgiving,
that's what
it's about.
nnot afford to govern out of anger...”
– Barack Obama, Address to Congress 2/24/09
“...you're not strong by putting other people down –
you're strong by lifting them up.”
– Barack Obama, Chicago IL 6/15/08
“Strong countries and strong Presidents talk
to their adversaries as well as their friends...”
– Barack Obama, Denver, CO 1/30/08
“...we learned to disagree without being disagreeable...
so long as we are willing to listen to each other, we can
assume the best in people instead of the worst.”
– Barack Obama, Springfield, IL 2/10/07
“...what people often note as my even temperament I think
draws from Hawaii....there just is a cultural bias toward
courtesy and trying to work through problems in a way
that makes everybody feel like they're being listened to.”
– Barack Obama, U.S. News & World Report 5/30/08
“We need a President... as the defender of
fairness and opportunity for every American.”
– Barack Obama, Cedar Rapids, IA 7/30/07

Our President is just one man,
But he has given us hope that, "Yes, we can."

We can treat each other as family, or ʻohana,
And take more responsibility, kuleana.

We can work to make things right, or pono.
And show our respect by saying mahalo.

We can be smarter, more akamai.
We can find agreement, lōkahi, if we try.

We can preserve, protect, mālama,
and give our kōkua to President Obama!

"...I can't do this on my own. I need your help."
– Barack Obama, Washington D.C. 7/8/08

And if we all work together very hard,
maybe our President will have a **lū‘au**
in his big backyard!

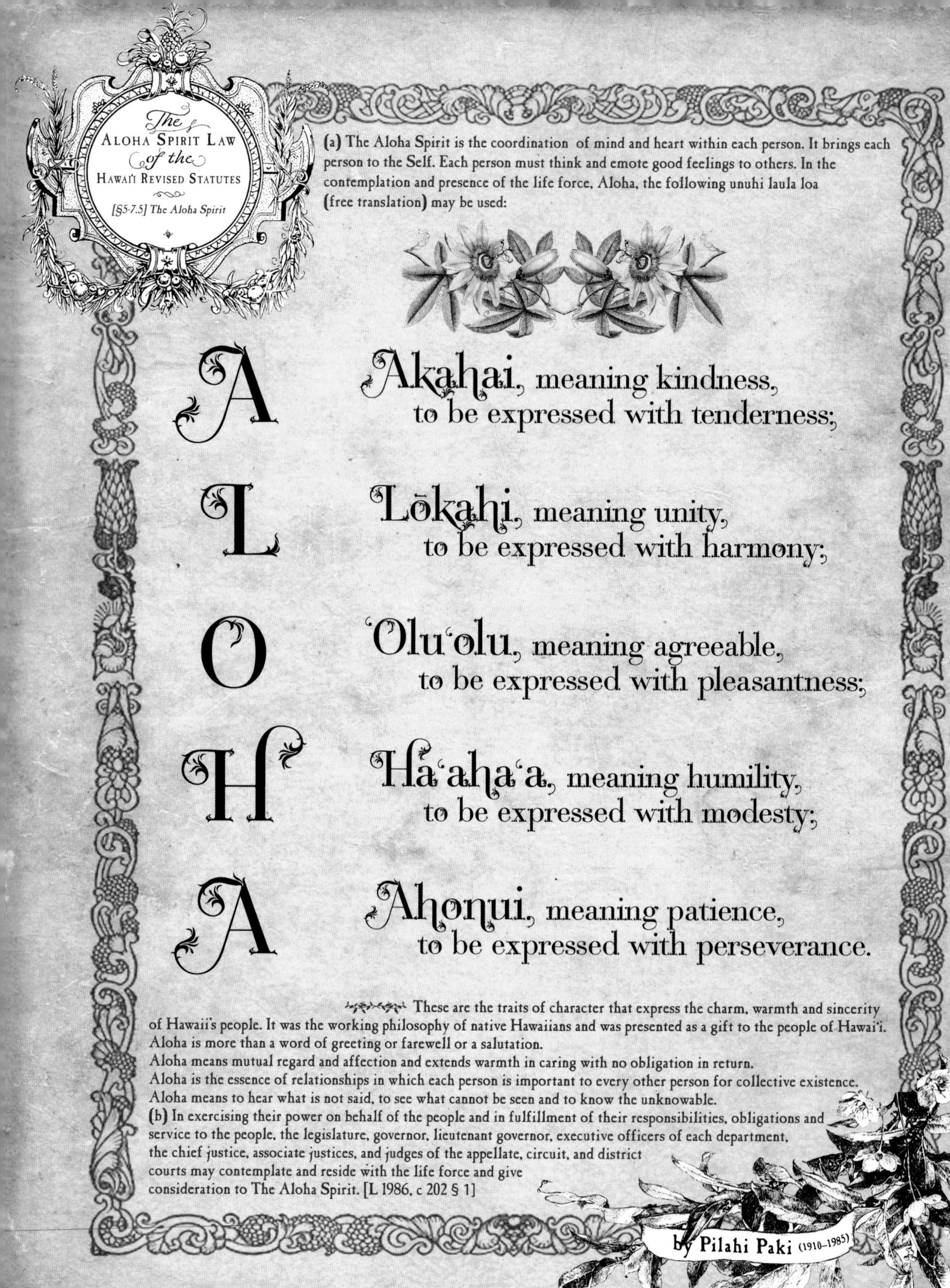
The Aloha Spirit Law of the Hawai'i Revised Statutes
[§5-7.5] The Aloha Spirit
(a) The Aloha Spirit is the coordination of mind and heart within each person. It brings each person to the Self. Each person must think and emote good feelings to others. In the contemplation and presence of the life force, Aloha, the following unuhi laula loa (free translation) may be used:
A
L
O
H
A
Akahai, meaning kindness, to be expressed with tenderness;
Lōkahi, meaning unity, to be expressed with harmony;
'Olu'olu, meaning agreeable, to be expressed with pleasantness;
Ha'aha'a, meaning humility, to be expressed with modesty;
Ahonui, meaning patience, to be expressed with perseverance.
These are the traits of character that express the charm, warmth and sincerity of Hawaii's people. It was the working philosophy of native Hawaiians and was presented as a gift to the people of Hawai'i.
Aloha is more than a word of greeting or farewell or a salutation.
Aloha means mutual regard and affection and extends warmth in caring with no obligation in return.
Aloha is the essence of relationships in which each person is important to every other person for collective existence.
Aloha means to hear what is not said, to see what cannot be seen and to know the unknowable.
(b) In exercising their power on behalf of the people and in fulfillment of their responsibilities, obligations and service to the people, the legislature, governor, lieutenant governor, executive officers of each department, the chief justice, associate justices, and judges of the appellate, circuit, and district courts may contemplate and reside with the life force and give consideration to The Aloha Spirit. [L 1986, c 202 § 1]
by Pilahi Paki (1910–1985)

About the Narration & Music

Narrated by: Amy Hanaiali'i
These Islands Performed by: Amy Hanaiali'i
Obama Mele Composition & Slack Key Guitar: Keli'i Kāneali'i
Hawaiian Blessing Oli (chant) by: Healani Youn
Aloha Spirit Oli (chant) Performed by: Keli'i Kāneali'i & Healani Youn

For additional music credits please see following page.

Amy Hanaiali'i

Three-time GRAMMY® Award Nominee for Best Hawaiian Music Album and winner of 12 Nā Hōkū Hanohano Awards, Amy Hanaiali'i is one of Hawaii's most prominent performers. She began singing almost before she could walk, and comes from a family of famous Hawaiian entertainers. Her grandmother and musical mentor, Jennie Napua Hanaiali'i Woodd, was one of the original Royal Hawaiian Girls during the 1930s and '40s and the choreographer for numerous Hollywood motion pictures filmed during that time. Her grandmother encouraged her to master *ha'i* (female falsetto singing) and Amy's resurrection of this style has won her the hearts of many. When Amy is not recording or touring she lives with her husband and daughter on their shrimp farm on the island of Moloka'i. Visit: www.myspace.com/amyhanaialii

Keli'i Kāneali'i

Keli'i Kāneali'i began singing at the age of six with his church choir. Born and raised on 'Oahu, he is the youngest of 15 children. Keli'i was a founding member and former lead vocalist for the music group *HAPA*. After 18 years with *HAPA*, during which time he was awarded six Nā Hōkū Hanohano Awards, Keli'i left to pursue his solo career. When Keli'i is not recording or performing his contemporary ballads, traditional Hawaiian songs and sharing his aloha around the world, he enjoys spending time in his garden on the island of Kaua'i where he lives with his wife and sons. Keli'i says he gets his song writing inspiration while working with the land.
Visit: www.keliikanealii.com

Dr. Carolan was born in Melbourne, Australia. He moved to Hawai'i in 1977. He has been a pediatrician in private practice on the island of Kaua'i, Hawai'i since 1979. He has four sons and one granddaughter.

Joanna F. Carolan was born in San Francisco, California. Her grandparents moved to Kaua'i in 1967; she spent part of her teenage years living with them in Wailua. She is an artist and owner of Banana Patch Studio & Gallery on Kaua'i.

Other Dr. Carolan books available from Banana Patch Press:

Ten Days in Hawaii, A Counting Book

B is for Beach, An Alphabet Book

Where Are My Slippers? A Book of Colors

Goodnight Hawaiian Moon

Old Makana Had a Taro Farm

This is My Piko

For more information visit:
www.bananapatchpress.com
www.bananapatchstudio.com

Acknowledgements & Additional Credits

Additional Credits for the Narration & Oli:
Keli'i Kaneali'i appears courtesy of Mountain Apple Company, www.mountainapplecompany.com
Amy's Narration recorded by: Tony Hugar, www.audioresourcehonolulu.com
Pahu Drum & Ipu Heke (double gourd drum): Healani Youn
Obama Mele & Oli Produced by: Keli'i Kaneali'i & Ron Pendragon
Mixed & Mastered by: Ron Pendragon, www.fattuesdayrecords.com
Executive Producer: Banana Patch Press

Additional Credits for *These Islands*:
Music and Lyrics by: Danny Couch
Arrangement by: Matt Catingub
Mixed by: Matt Catingub at Bugntac Studios
Recorded at: Avex Studios Hawaii
Recording Engineer: Milan Bertosa
Hawaiian Translation by: Adrian K. Kamali'i
Keyboards: Matt Catingub
Guitars: Jeff Peterson & David 'Chino' Montero
Bass: Steve Jones
Produced By: Allen Sviridoff and Matt Catingub

Additional Text & Art Credits:
Contributing Editors: Healani Youn and Mary Nissenson
Graphic Design Contribution: Robin Pearl Graphics, Robin Pearl & Kim Busch-French
Additional Graphic Design: Kauai's Printmaker, Tom Niblick
Additional Graphics: IstockPhoto.com, ClipArt.com

Photo Credits:
Back Cover: Tom Niblick (Hanalei Sunset), Stewart Fern (Diamond Head sailboats)
Front End Sheet: J.D. Griggs (volcano); Polynesian Cultural Center (hula dancers); Gonçalo Veiga (turtle); Robin Pearl Graphics (Hawaii map); Misuzu Nordmeier (Diamond Head sunrise); Dr. Louis Herman (whale)
Back end Sheet: Misuzu Nordmeier (Diamond Head); AP Photo/Marco Garcia (Obama & daughters); AP Photo/Pablo Martinez Monsivais (Obama "shaka"); Glenn Schot (shaka cats); MCC Eric A Clement, USN (Obama jumpshot); James Bowman (Obamas dancing)
Page 4: AP Photo/Alex Brandon (Obama bodysurfing Sandy Beach); Ildar Sagdejev (yield sign)
Page 6: AP Photo/Elaine Thompson (Obama with orchid lei); Wayne "Bastian" Worthington Jr. (Duke statue)
Page 16: Laura Kong (Obama lay-up 1979 Hawai'i State Basketball Championship)
Page 17: AP Photo/Alex Brandon (Obama bodysurfing Sandy Beach)
Page 19: Joe Wrinn/Harvard News Office (Obama at Harvard Law Library) disclaimer: Harvard University & Punahou School are not affiliated with Banana Patch Press and do not endorse this book
Page 22: Honolulu Advertiser & Star Bulletin newspaper headlines used with permission
Page 30: Maka Herrod (Kupuna stringing a flower lei)
Page 34/35: Wayne "Bastian" Worthington, Jr. (church photos)
Page 35: AP Photo/Nam Y. Huh (Obama at prayer)
Page 40 & 41: Getty Images and Corbis Images (children, except Obama)
Page 44: Save Our Seas (The Reef is Alive Poster) www.saveourseas.org
Page 44/45: Nancy Forbes (Honu Family, watercolor); Angela Ditmer (Hawaiian Monk Seal)
Page 51: Bebe, Kauai Fine Art (Hukilau) www.brunias.com
Page 52/52: Jupiter Images (rainbow)
Page 60: AP Photo/Governor's Office Hawaii (Obama shaka – derivative work)
Note: all family photographs of Barack Obama used with permission (back cover, ends sheets, and inside pages: 1, 3, 16, 18, 36, 39 & 41)

Mahalo To:
Donn & Nancy Forbes, Mark Bernstein, Andy Winer, Senator Gary Hooser, Mayor Maryanne Kusaka, Michael Ceurvorst, Roger Jellinek, Amy Hammond, Booklines Hawaii; Jeff, Elisa, Bev, Kerry, and their team, Wikimedia, and special thanks to all the Banana Patch Team: Sheri, Jana, Alice, Naomi, Michelle, Erin, Angela, Shanelle, Brooks, Mitzi, Patty, Liselle, Anna, Crystal, Patricia, Marjanne, Karl, Dennis, Terry, Mary, Brandee & Schar.

UA MAU KE EA O KA AINA I KA PONO
State Motto: Ua mau ke ea o ka aina i ka pono
The life of the land is perpetuated in righteousness
Mount Wai'ale'ale on the island of Kaua'i is considered to be one of the wettest spots on earth, with an average rainfall of over 426 inches per year. The record rainfall was 683 inches recorded in 1982. Wai'ale'ale means "rippling water".
The State Flower of Hawai'i is the Yellow Hibiscus.